sushi

by Ryuichi Yoshii,
Brigid Treloar and Hideo Dekura

TUTTLE PUBLISHING
Tokyo • Rutland, Vermont • Singapore

Published by Tuttle Publishing, an imprint of Periplus
Editions, with editorial offices at 130 Joo Seng Road,
#06-01, Singapore 368357, and 364 Innovation Drive,
North Clarendon, VT 05759, USA.

ISBN 10: 0-8048-3846-1
ISBN 13: 978-0-8048-3846-7
Printed in Malaysia

Distributed by
North America, Latin America and Europe
Tuttle Publishing, 364 Innovation Drive,
North Clarendon, VT 05759-9436.
Tel: (802) 773-8930 Fax: (802) 773-6993
info@tuttlepublishing.com
www.tuttlepublishing.com

Japan
Tuttle Publishing, Yaekari Building 3F,
5-4-12 Osaki, Shinagawa-ku, Tokyo 141-0032.
Tel: (03) 5437-0171 Fax: (03) 5437-0755
tuttle-sales@gol.com

Asia Pacific
Berkeley Books Pte Ltd.
130 Joo Seng Road #06-01
Singapore 368357.
Tel: (65) 6280-1330 Fax: (65) 6280-6290
inquiries@periplus.com.sg
www.periplus.com

10 09 08 07
5 4 3 2

TUTTLE PUBLISHING® is a registered trademark of Tuttle Publishing,
a division of Periplus Editions (HK) Ltd.

Contents

Introducing Sushi

The Japanese believe that food should satisfy all the senses. Their food is always prepared with great care, using the freshest ingredients in ways that delight both the eyes and the taste buds. The enormous number of sushi restaurants outside Japan attests to the popularity of this appetizing food.

Fish and rice make up the staple diet of the Japanese people. Sashimi, which means "raw" in Japanese, is usually served as an appetizer. (Sashimi generally refers to the delicately arranged slices of raw seafood and fresh fish that are served with soy and other dipping sauces.) Sushi, pronounced "zushi" when it follows another word ending in a vowel, is either the main course or the next-to-last dish in a Japanese dinner, served prior to dessert. Sushi consists of slightly sweet, vinegar-flavored rice either topped with seafood, egg or vegetables, or rolled with a variety of fillings inside dark green sheets of toasted nori seaweed. Wasabi, a spicy mustard-like condiment, pickled ginger (*gari*), and soy sauce are usually served with sushi. Miso soup may also be served with sushi.

To eat sushi, use your chopsticks (or fingers) to pick up a piece of sushi and dip the end of the topping into the soy sauce. (Do not dip the rice in the soy sauce as you will taste only soy, not the delicate flavors of the topping and rice.) Put the sushi in your mouth with the topping side down, so that the topping meets your taste buds. Before eating another piece of sushi, eat a slice of pickled ginger to clean your palate, and have a sip of tea. Japanese green tea removes the oiliness of fish. Nowadays, people also drink beer, wine or sake, the traditional Japanese wine made from fermented rice, with sushi.

Sushi is a simple, light and healthy food. Raw fish and fresh seafood contain many vitamins and minerals, a high amount of health-giving omega-3 fatty acids, and little cholesterol. Rice has plenty of dietary fiber and no oil is added. There is an enormous variety of sushi in terms of shapes and ingredients. This makes sushi so complicated that it takes years for a professional chef to master all the technique, although the basic types of sushi are easy enough to be created at home by you with only a little bit of practice.

Equipment and Utensils

Bamboo rolling mat (*makisu*) This simple rolling mat used for making sushi rolls is made of thin strips of bamboo woven together with cotton string. After you have used the mat, scrub it down with a brush and dry it thoroughly, otherwise it may become moldy. It is best to buy an all-purpose mat measuring 12 x 12 in (30 x 30 cm), but smaller ones are also available. When making sushi, the mat must be dry.

Bowl with lid A large bowl with a lid is needed for holding the cooked sushi rice once it has been prepared, to keep it warm. An insulated bowl or electric rice cooker pot is ideal.

Chopping board A chopping board is needed for a variety of tasks, from preparing fish and vegetables to assembling all the different sorts of sushi. A wooden chopping board always used to be used for sushi making, but now resin boards are widely available and are easier to keep free of odors. It is best to have a board measuring at least 10 x 15 in (25 x 38 cm).

Cooking chopsticks (*saibashi*) The chopsticks used for cooking are two to three times longer than normal chopsticks used for eating. Cooking chopsticks are extremely useful implements, once you have mastered the technique, as they enable you to manipulate food using only one hand. You will also want to have several pairs of chopsticks for individual use at the table when eating sushi and sashimi.

Fan (*uchiwa*) An uchiwa is a flat fan made of paper or silk stretched over light bamboo ribs, and is traditionally used for cooling the sushi rice as you add the vinegar dressing. While it is delightful to own an *uchiwa*, a piece of heavy paper or cardboard will do the job just as well.

Fish scaler When cleaning and preparing fish at home, it is easiest to use a scaler, available from a fish market. Simply draw it up the body of the fish, working from tail to head. Do not use the back of a cleaver as a substitute, as you run the risk of bruising the fish.

Grater Sushi chefs use a length of sharkskin for grating wasabi root; for grating pieces of ginger and daikon, they use a ceramic bowl that has small teeth on the surface. If you are using a straightforward household grater, a flat one made of stainless steel with very fine teeth is most suitable. Be sure to choose one that is comfortable to hold and has closely packed, sharp teeth. When using the grater, particularly when grating ginger, use a circular motion.

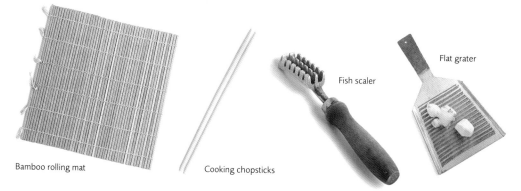

Flat grater

Fish scaler

Bamboo rolling mat

Cooking chopsticks

Knives Japanese chefs use knives that are traditionally made from the same steel used to make samurai swords. The best sort of knife to use for filleting fish and for slicing pieces of fish for sashimi and sushi is a long, slender one with a pointed end. A wide, heavy knife is useful for cutting through bone, as when removing a fish's head. Never use a serrated knife when cutting fish, as it will tear the flesh. For chopping and slicing vegetables, a long, square-ended cleaver is best. Look after your knives and either sharpen them on a whetstone or have them sharpened by a professional. Sushi chefs keep a damp cloth nearby, to wipe the knives clean from time to time while they work.

Rice cooling tub (*hangiri*) The broad, wooden hangiri, generally made of cypress, has low sides and is designed specifically for cooling sushi rice. This gives the rice the ideal texture and gloss, but a glass or ceramic flat-bottomed bowl can be substituted instead. The bigger the bowl the better, as you will then be able to stir and separate the rice grains properly. If you are using a *hangiri*, wash it well after use, dry it carefully, then wrap it in a cloth and store it face downward in a cool, dry place.

Rice cooker An electric rice cooker is highly recommended for cooking rice, as it will control the temperature and cooking time to give perfect rice every time. Otherwise, you can use a heavy pot with a tight-fitting lid.

Serving plates When serving sushi, you need a set of plates that are as flat as possible. If the serving plate is curved or ridged, as is common with Western-style crockery, the presentation of the sushi will not be as attractive and the top-heavy pieces of sushi may fall over.

Square omelette pan A square-shaped omelette pan about 1 in (3 cm) deep is traditionally used for making sushi omelettes. A thick pan that retains heat is ideal, but can be heavy to handle. You can substitute a conventional round skillet about 10 in (25 cm) in diameter and trim the sides of the omelette once it has been cooked to make it square.

Tweezers Heavy, straight-ended tweezers come in handy for deboning fish. These are obtainable from a fish market.

Wooden rice paddle (*shamoji*) A wooden rice paddle, called a *shamoji*, is traditionally used for turning and spreading sushi rice when cooling it, but any kind of broad, flat spatula will do the job. You can use a large wooden spoon or a wooden spatula. Because wood tends to absorb flavors, it is best to use your chosen spoon exclusively for sushi rice. Before using a wooden spoon for sushi rice, wet it thoroughly, or the rice will stick to it.

Tweezers for deboning fish

Rice cooling tub (*hangiri*) and
wooden rice paddle (*shamoji*)

Square omelette pan

Heavy chopping cleaver and
long, thin filleting knife

Sushi Ingredients

Bonito flakes (*katsuo boshi*) are sandy brown flakes of smoked, dried and fermented bonito fish that are used to make **dashi**, which is the basic Japanese soup stock. For household use, instant *dashi* powder or granules (*hon-dashi*) can be used—simply add to boiling water to make *dashi* stock.

Eel is not widely available fresh outside of Japan—much of it worldwide is exported to Japan where it is made into *unagi*—barbequed eel. *Unagi* is steamed and then broiled, after being brushed with soy sauce and mirin. You can find prepared *unagi* in the refrigerated sections of Asian supermarkets.

togarashi) is sold in small bottles and contains a mixture of dried chili pepper, black pepper and other spices. Do not use other forms of chili powder as substitutes, as they will probably be too strong.

Japanese cucumbers are much smaller and thinner than normal cucumbers—about 6–8 in (15–20 cm) long. They are less watery and have fewer seeds, a firmer flesh and softer skins. If you can't find them, use pickling gherkins or baby cucumbers. Buy firm-skinned cucumbers with a medium green color. Cut into 2–4 in (5–10 cm) lengths before slicing. Cucumber is often used as a filling in sushi rolls and as a garnish or ingredient in salads.

Daikon radish is a Japanese white radish that looks and tastes like a bland carrot and is usually at least 15 in (40 cm) long. Look for firm, shiny ones with smooth skin and straight leaves. Peel them deep enough to remove the skin and outer layer of fibers beneath it. Cut into 2–4 in (5–10 cm) sections before slicing. Daikon contains various enzymes and is good for the digestion when eating strongly flavored or oily foods.

Enoki mushrooms have long, thin stalks and tiny caps. Choose ones that are crisp and white; yellowish brown ones are old and should be avoided. Cut off the "roots" at the bottom of the stalks.

Japanese chili powder (*ichimi*

Japanese eggplants are similar to other Asian eggplants—longer, thinner and smaller than Mediterranean (globe) eggplants. They are usually 8–12 in (20–30 cm) long and 2–3 in (5–8 cm) in diameter. Choose firm, purple, smooth-fleshed ones with straight stalks. Eggplants are sliced, then lightly grilled or fried before being used in sushi.

Japanese green tea (*ocha*) is the perfect accompaniment to sushi as it cleanses the palate. It is available in leaf and powdered form or in teabags. There are various types of green tea, so follow the instructions on the packets.

Kamaboko is a Japanese-style fish cake, available fresh or frozen. There are various forms, some of them dyed pink. *Kamaboko* can be used in Chirashi Sushi (page 70).

Kampyo is dried bottle gourd or calabash, used in the form of shavings or ribbonlike strips. Before being used in sushi, kampyo is tenderized and seasoned (page 75).

Kimchee is a Korean spicy fermented cabbage. Kimchee is strongly flavored, so use only a small quantity.

Kombu is dried sea kelp, a type of seaweed. This sea vegetable is available dried in the form of hard, flat, black sheets that have a fine white powder on the surface. *Kombu* is used to flavor *dashi*, the basic soup stock, and sushi rice. Wipe the surface of the sheets with a damp cloth before use to remove the powder (do not wash the kombu as that will remove its flavor). Avoid *kombu* that is wrinkled and thin.

Lotus root (*renkon*) is the crunchy root of the lotus plant, which is used in a variety of

Japanese dishes, including Chirashi Sushi. It is peeled, then sliced before cooking. The slices resemble white wheels with holes in them. The root discolors as soon as it is cut, so place the slices in water with 1 teaspoon vinegar to avoid this. Fresh lotus roots are available in Asian markets either packed in mud, or washed and packed in plastic.

Mirin is a sweet alcoholic wine made from rice. Store in a cool, dark place after opening. If mirin is unavailable, use 1 teaspoon sugar mixed with 1 tablespoon sake or sherry in place of 1 tablespoon mirin.

Miso is a fermented paste of mashed soybeans, salt and water with a fermenting agent—usually soy "koji," rice or barley. There are many types of miso, but they can be broadly divided into three categories: sweet, nonsweet and salty. **White miso**, the sweetest, is ivory to yellow in color and is seldom available outside Japan. **Red miso** is aged the longest and is the salty form; it is actually brown rather than red. White and red miso, plus many other blends, are available in Asian supermarkets.

Shiitake mushrooms

black Chinese mushrooms

Nori is a type of dried seaweed that comes in large green sheets that are used for making sushi rolls. It is sold in plastic packets of 10 to 20 sheets which usually measure 8 x 7 in (20 x 17 cm). Buy toasted nori, known as yaki-nori, which is dark green. But in any case, it is a good idea to lightly toast the nori on both sides over an open flame before using it. Once the wrapping has been opened, use the nori as soon as possible or store it in an airtight container in a cool place.

Rice used for sushi is always short-grain Japanese white rice. Use Japanese rice or California short-grain rice. The size, consistency, taste and smell of other types of rice are not suitable for making sushi.

Sake is a type of Japanese rice wine with a delicate, sweet flavor. Sake is used in cooking to tenderize meat and fish, and to make ingredients more flavorful. It also counteracts acidity. Buy cooking sake (*ryori sake*) or inexpensive drinking sake for making sushi.

Shiitake mushrooms are sold fresh or dried (the dried ones are usually known as **black Chinese mushrooms**). Fresh shiitake should be plump with dark brown caps, cleanly tucked edges and white gills underneath. Remove and discard the tough ends of the stems. They taste best when lightly grilled. Use a knife to score an asterisk pattern on the caps, but avoid cutting through them. This allows even cooking and looks decorative. Soak dried shiitake mushrooms in water for 30 minutes before using. The longer they are soaked, the softer they become. Good-quality shiitake mushrooms should become fleshy and plump after soaking.

Pickled ginger (*gari*) is slices of ginger that have been pickled in salt and sweet vinegar. They are a delicate pink to tan color and are available in bottles and packets, or you can make your own (page 25). The bright red vinegared ginger is not used with sushi. Small amounts of *gari* are eaten between bites of sushi to freshen the palate.

Sesame seeds (*goma*) are normally lightly toasted before use. You can buy them toasted or you can toast them yourself in a dry pan over medium heat, moving them around so that they turn golden brown but do not burn. Black sesame seeds are used as a garnish for cuttlefish and are sometimes used for sushi decoration.

Shiso is an aromatic leaf that is a member of the mint family and is known as perilla in the West. Buy fresh, green leaves. There is also a red variety that is used for coloring and flavoring *umeboshi* and other Japanese pickles. This leaf is also widely used in Vietnamese cooking.

Snow pea sprouts are available from produce stores and are sold in packets to prevent them from being crushed and keep them fresh.

Soboro is a ground ingredient made from white fish meat that has been boiled, pickled into fiber and dried. It is used in Chirashi Sushi (page 75). You can buy it readymade, in a jar.

Soy sauce (*shoyu*) is a salty condiment made from soybeans and used both as an ingredient and as a table condiment. Dark soy sauce is thicker and often less salty than light soy sauce. Low-sodium products are also available. Japanese soy is more suitable for sushi, as it is naturally fermented and less salty than Chinese soy.

Sushi vinegar (*awasezu*) is a mild-tasting vinegar made from rice, as are other Japanese vinegars. It is specifically made for sushi. Normal Chinese or Japanese rice vinegar may also be used, however the quantity may need to be reduced by a quarter so the rice is not too sour.

Tofu is a white curd made from soybean milk. The Japanese "silken" variety has a soft, glossy surface. It is softer and smoother than Chinese tofu. Fresh tofu must be kept in the refrigerator. Once opened, it should be kept in a tub of water.

Tofu pouches (*aburage*) are thinly sliced deep-fried tofu, which form pockets when one side is cut and opened. They are sold in Japanese or Asian food stores, normally in plastic packets of 16 pieces. Canned or frozen tofu pouches are also available. The canned variety is usually already seasoned in sweetened soy sauce and sliced. Tofu pouches are often used to make Inari Sushi and added to udon noodle dishes.

Wakame is another type of seaweed that is available in dried form. It must be reconstituted under running water and is used to flavor miso soup.

Wasabi is a Japanese form of horseradish. Wasabi roots are olive green with a bumpy skin. The best roots are 4–5 years old, 4–6 inches (10–15 cm) long, and should be fat and moist. Fresh wasabi is expensive and largely unavailable outside Japan, so powdered or paste formulations are commonly used. Wasabi powder is mixed with a small amount of tepid water to make a paste, but prepare only a small quantity at a time as its potency diminishes quickly.

Sushi Decorations

It is traditional to decorate sushi plates with leaves or vegetables cut into delicate shapes and patterns. These can be elaborate or simple, and many different ingredients may be used—including camellia and ivy leaves, shiso and bamboo leaves; carved pieces of cucumber or carrot; mounds of wasabi in various shapes, and mounds of finely shredded seaweed, diakon radish or carrot. In many restaurants, plastic cutouts are used, but you can make your own decorations using real leaves that are available from your garden. Draw your chosen design onto the leaf and use a small, sharp pointed knife to cut it out. Some traditional designs are shown below.

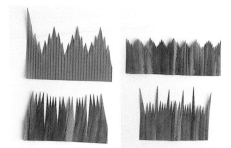

Leaf decorations
The grasslike cutouts placed in between the pieces of sushi, like walls, are named **sekisho**, after the borders between townships.

Cucumber trees
1 Cut a 2 x 1-in (5 x 2^1/$_2$-cm) rectangle from the side of a small Japanese cucumber, about ^{1}/$_4$ in (6 mm) thick. It should have skin on one side.
2 Cut an odd number of slices about ^{3}/$_4$ of the way down the length of the rectangle, each about ^{1}/$_8$ in (3 mm) apart, leaving the bottom ^{1}/$_2$ in (12 mm) uncut.
3 Leaving the outermost slices, curl each alternate slice down into the base of the cucumber with your fingers as shown in the photograph.

Varieties of leaf cut-outs

Ginger rose

Radish cups

Cucumber curls

Simple leaf garnish

Carrot petals

1 Peel and slice a carrot into 1-in (2$^1/_2$-cm) lengths, using the thick end of the carrot, not the thin end. Stand each length on one end.
2 Cut a strip of paper $^1/_2$ x 2 in (12 mm x 5 cm) and fold it into a pentagon as shown.
3 Place a folded pentagon on top of each and use it as a template to trim the sides of the carrot into the shape of a pentagon. Remove the paper and further trim the sides to form a star as shown.
4 Slice each star into thin star-shaped petals.

Wasabi leaf

Wasabi is usually served in a small mound on a plate or even shaped into a leaf—the vein pattern on top is drawn with a toothpick. When eating sashimi, you can add wasabi to the soy sauce or just pick up a small amount of wasabi at the same time as you pick up the pieces of raw food.

Selecting Sushi Seafood

The freshest seafood makes the best sushi, for reasons of health, taste and beauty. If you can, purchase your fish from the market, and always buy whatever is in season. Most fish can be eaten raw, but it is best to choose fish that are commonly used in sushi. Remember, keep all seafood refrigerated until needed.

Whole fish

Whenever possible, buy fish whole and fillet them at home. You can then be sure that the meat is fresh. Use the following guidelines to ensure that the fish are fresh.
- Check that the eyes are plump, clear and bright. Avoid fish with cloudy pupils.
- The gills should be bright pink-red and look moist. If fish is not fresh, the gills are black-red.
- Overall, the coloring of the fish should be bright or lustrous.
- Stroke the fish to ensure that the flesh is firm and elastic. Stale fish are less elastic and may feel sticky.
- The fish should have a "clean" smell. Avoid ones that have a strong fishy odor.
- Mackerel should have a pointed shape to their stomachs, and the tail on both mackerel and bonito should be upright. A drooping tail shows that a fish is not fresh.

Fish fillets

With bigger fish, it may be inconvenient or uneconomical to buy a whole fish, so buy fillets and smaller cuts. When buying only a portion of a fish, use the following guidelines.
- Fillets should be moist and have a good color.
- White fish should look almost transparent.
- Cut tuna should have distinct stripes in it around the belly but be clear red without any stripes in other parts.
- The head end of the fish is more tender than the tail end.
- With most fish, the back is the most delicious part. Tuna and swordfish are exceptions, in that the tender, fatty belly area is most sought-after.

Other seafood
- When buying shrimp, if they are alive they should be active and of good color. If they are no longer alive, check that the stripes are distinct: they should not be blurred together.
- Touch the tentacles of squid and check that the suckers are still active. The skin around the eyes should be clear blue.
- Sea urchins should be yellow or orange, firm and not slimy.
- Live shellfish are best. When you gently open the shell, it should close by itself.

Filleting Fish at Home

Types of seafood cuts for sushi

Most fish cuts are suitable for sushi. The fish pieces may be raw, grilled or preserved in vinegar. Fresh raw fish for sushi include salmon, snapper, king fish, yellowtail and tuna.

Shellfish is also suitable. Most shrimp are cooked before being used as sushi toppings. Fresh lobster has a wonderful texture and a natural sweetness that makes it very suitable for sushi, though it may be too expensive for everyday use. You may prepare a lobster yourself, or purchase fresh or frozen lobster tails, for use in sushi.

Eel is available filleted and barbecued with sweet soy sauce from the refrigerated or frozen-food section of most Japanese and some other Asian markets. Before using as a sushi topping, steam the eel or heat it gently in the microwave, then slice into sushi-sized pieces.

Mackerel is the most popular fish for preserving in vinegar as a sushi topping. In one region of Japan, rice and mackerel sushi are wrapped in Japanese persimmon leaves to enhance the flavor.

Tasty fish eggs, such as caviar, salmon roe, *tobikko* (flying fish roe) and sea urchin roe, add a dramatic decorative effect to sushi, as well as a distinctive taste sensation.

Nowadays, even processed fish products are becoming popular, such as processed crabmeat (*kani kamaboko*) which is a common ingredient used in California rolls and hand rolls or sushi cones. Also, canned fish such as tuna, mixed with Japanese mayonnaise, is quite popular among the youth of Japan.

Step-by-step fish filleting

In this filleting illustration (opposite), a king fish is used. The utensils needed are a cutting board, a sharp filleting knife and a clean kitchen towel. Other medium-sized fish, such as snapper, salmon or bonito, may be substituted for king fish.

Fish such as snapper must be scaled before filleting. If scaling is required, wipe the knife occasionally with a clean cloth to avoid shredding the flesh.

This three-part filleting process yields two fish fillets. The skeleton and tail are discarded.

1 Place the fish on a board. With a sharp filleting knife, slit open its belly, remove the viscera and then rinse it under running water. Pat the fish dry with a clean cloth or kitchen towel. Holding the fish head with your left hand, place the knife behind the gills and cut halfway through the head; but do not remove the head.

2 With one hand holding the fish firmly, start cutting the fillet from head to tail along the backbone of the fish, lifting the fillet away as you cut. Place the cut fillet aside, then turn the fish over and fillet the other side.

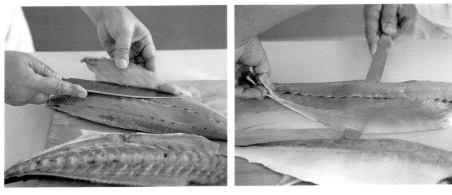

3 Trim away any remaining bones in the cut fillets or around the visceral area.

4 To skin the fillets, place each fillet skin side down on the board. Then insert a knife between the skin and flesh at the tail end, and move the knife toward the head end while holding the skin. Discard the skin.

Sushi Fish Cuts

For both sashimi and sushi, fish fillets should be deboned, scaled and, where necessary, skinned. The parts of the fish that are not usable for sashimi and sushi may be used in many other ways, such as the spine for making stock.

You will generally need to cut fish fillets into smaller blocks before making sashimi and sushi slices. The length of the block will depend on the fish being used, but it should be rectangular in shape, measuring about 3 in (7 cm) across and $1^1/_2$ in (4 cm) thick. The resulting sushi and sashimi slices should be $^1/_4$ to $^1/_2$ in ($^1/_2$ to 1 cm) thick. Remember that the slices and resulting sushi should be small enough to fit easily in your mouth.

Angled cuts are used to slice raw fish such as tuna or salmon for sushi and sashimi.

Straight cuts are used to slice raw fish for sashimi.

When cutting fish for sushi, always cut with the knife pulling the slice toward you. The flesh should be sliced on the bias along the length of the fish or the fillet to give the best results texturally, visually and for taste. One of the basic cutting techniques is the angled cut, known as *sorigiri*.

Start with a rectangular block of fish about the width of your hand, about 3 in (7 cm) across and $1^1/_2$ in (4 cm) high. With a large fish, such as tuna, you will be able to cut a block like this from the larger fillet that you purchased from the market. With other fish, such as salmon, try to cut the fish into a block, although the ends and sides may not be particularly even. With salmon or white fish, you can often cut the slices following the existing angle of the fillet.

First slice a triangular piece about $1^1/_2$ in (4 in) from one end of the block to make an angled edge to work with. (Any scraps can be used in rolled sushi.) Then, slanting your knife at the same angle, cut slices that are about $1/_4-1/_2$ in (6 mm–1 cm) thick. The remaining piece at the other end will also be triangular.

This method is also used with smaller filleted fish, adjusting the knife angle to suit the fillet. With fish such as tuna, the resulting slices will be uniform and rectangular. With smaller fillets, you may have triangular edges or thinner slices. Sometimes you may need to use more than one slice for a piece of Nigiri Sushi.

Sashimi Cuts

Straight cut: Using a squared-off edge of filleted fish block, cut $1/_4$-in (6-mm) slices straight down along the fillet. With tuna, the slices need to be a little thicker than for some other fish because the flesh is likely to break up along the lines if the slices are thin.

Cubic cut for tuna: Slice straight down through the fish, making $1/_2-1$-in (12 mm–$2^1/_2$-cm) thick slices, then cut the slices into cubes of the same width.

Fine-strip cut for white fish or squid: Cut $1/_4$-in ($1/_2$-cm) straight slices from the fillet. Lay each slice flat and cut them lengthwise into strips $1/_2$ in (6 mm) wide.

Paper-thin slicing for white fish: Measure about $1^1/_2$ in (4 cm) from the top of the block of fish and slice off a triangular piece to make an angled edge to work with. Then steadily use your knife to cut paper-thin slices at an angle along the fillet. With many white fish, the resulting slices are almost transparent.

Cooking Rice for Sushi

The first step in making sushi is to prepare the rice. It is well worth buying an electric rice cooker, as it reduces the process of cooking the rice to the simple press of a button. The following method is for Japanese-style rice, to which a vinegar dressing is later added (see opposite page).

1$^1/_2$ cups (375 g) uncooked short-grain Japanese rice
1$^1/_2$ cups (375 ml) water
1 tablespoon mirin or sake

1 Using a measuring cup, measure the required amount of rice and place it into a bowl that holds at least twice the volume of the rice.

2 Wash the rice by adding water to the bowl. Stir the rice briskly for about 10 seconds, then cover it with your hand and carefully drain away the milky water. Repeat this process until the water runs clear. Transfer the rice to a fine-mesh sieve to drain. Set aside for 30 minutes.

3 Place all the ingredients and the washed rice in the electric rice cooker and allow the rice to soak for 20 to 30 minutes—the rice grains will absorb moisture and start to swell. Then switch on the rice cooker.

Note: If not using an electric rice cooker, place all the ingredients in a heavy saucepan. Soak the rice for 20 to 30 minutes, then bring to a boil over medium heat. Boil the rice for 1 to 2 minutes, then cover the pan tightly, reduce the heat to low and simmer for 10 to 20 minutes until cooked. Turn off the heat and allow the cooked rice to steam for 20 minutes before removing the lid.

Preparing Cooked Sushi Rice

After cooking the rice, you will need a wooden sushi bowl and rice paddle, or a large non-metallic mixing or salad bowl and a wooden spatula to make the sushi rice. Do not use metallic utensils as the vinegar used to make sushi rice can react with metal and cause an unpleasant taste.

4 tablespoons rice vinegar
2 tablespoons sugar
1 teaspoon salt
1 portion cooked Japanese rice
  (see opposite page)

Note: Do not refrigerate cooked sushi rice, as this causes the gluten to congeal and reduces the stickiness of the rice, making it hard to shape properly, as well as reducing the flavor. Prepared sushi rice will not keep until the next day.

Makes 4 cups (475 g) Prepared
  Sushi Rice
Preparation time: 15 mins +
  30 mins soaking
Cooking time: 25 mins

1 Prepare the sushi rice vinegar sauce by combining the rice vinegar, sugar and salt in a small saucepan and heat over low heat, stirring occasionally, until the sugar is dissolved. Remove from the heat and set aside to cool. To stop the vinegar from distilling off, set the bowl of vinegar in a cold water bath to speed up the cooling process.
2 Wipe the inside of a wooden bowl with a damp cloth to moisten it slightly, and moisten the rice paddle with water. Transfer the cooked rice to the wooden bowl while it is still hot using the rice paddle.
3 Slowly pour the sushi rice vinegar sauce evenly over the cooked rice, a little at a time, and mix it into the rice with quick cutting strokes (not stirring) of the paddle across the bowl to separate the rice grains and spread the rice out. At the same time, fan the rice to cool it quickly by using a hand-held fan or an electric fan set at low. This will give a glossy finish to the rice. Continue until the rice is lukewarm. It should take about 10 minutes to mix in the sushi rice vinegar sauce thoroughly.
4 Spread a damp muslin cloth or kitchen towel over the rice to keep it moist and cover the bowl until ready to use.

Sushi and Sashimi Condiments

Tosa Soy Sauce

3 tablespoons soy sauce
3 tablespoons bonito flakes
1 tablespoon sake
$1/2$ teaspoon mirin

Bring all the ingredients to a boil in a small saucepan, stirring constantly. Remove from the heat, strain through a fine sieve over a bowl, then set aside to cool.

Makes $1/4$ cup (60 ml)   Preparation time: 5 mins
Cooking time: 5 mins

Pickled Carrot and Diakon

1 carrot
3-in (8-cm) section of diakon
  radish
1 teaspoon salt
3 tablespoons rice vinegar
$1/2$ teaspoon Japanese soy sauce
$1/8$ teaspoon grated fresh ginger
2 teaspoons sugar

Makes 2 cups
Preparation time: 15 mins + 30 mins
  to marinate + 8 hours chilling

1 Peel and finely shred the carrot and diakon using a grater or mandolin, then place them in a large bowl. Sprinkle with the salt, mix well and set aside for 30 minutes. Gently squeeze out as much water as possible from the vegetables.
2 Combine all the other ingredients in a small bowl and stir until the sugar is dissolved, then pour it over the vegetables and toss to mix well.
3 Refrigerate the pickles for 8 hours before serving.

Note: This pickle will keep for 1 week if refrigerated in an airtight container. For a quick variation, soak shredded carrot and diakon separately for 15 minutes in cold water, then drain well and sprinkle with sushi vinegar before serving.

Pickled Cucumber

1 Japanese cucumber, thinly sliced
2 teaspoons salt
4 tablespoons sushi vinegar

Makes $1/2$ cup
Preparation time: 5 mins + 5 mins
  to marinate + overnight chilling

1 Combine the cucumber slices with salt in a bowl and mix well. Set aside to marinate for 5 minutes.
2 Rinse the cucumber slices to remove the salt. Add the vinegar to the cucumber, mix well and chill in the refrigerator overnight before serving. If a milder vinegar flavor is preferred, heat the vinegar over medium heat for about 1 minute and allow to cool before using.

Pickled Ginger (Gari)

3 to 4 whole fresh ginger roots, peeled and thinly sliced along the grain
1 teaspoon salt, or to taste
$^1/_2$ cup (125 ml) rice vinegar
2 tablespoons sugar
$^1/_4$ cup (60 ml) water

Makes 1$^1/_2$ cups
Preparation time: 15 mins + 1 day to season
Cooking time: 30 seconds

1 Spread the ginger slices in a colander and rub with the salt. Set aside until soft, about 30 minutes or longer, then briefly blanch in boiling water. Remove the ginger slices from the heat, drain and cool.
2 Combine the rice vinegar, sugar and water in a small bowl and stir until the sugar is dissolved. Add to the ginger slices and toss well. Chill the pickles in the refrigerator for about 1 day until well seasoned.

Note: The ginger will turn slightly pinkish in the marinade. Pickled ginger will keep for several months if refrigerated in an airtight container. Allow 1 to 2 tablespoons per person for a sushi meal.

Sashimi

A wide variety of fish and seafood can be enjoyed as sashimi, allowing you to experience the full, natural flavor and texture of the fish in season. Sashimi means "raw" in Japanese.

Sashimi is sliced and prepared in various ways, depending on the texture of the ingredient being used, and then decoratively presented on a large platter garnished with shiso leaves, nori seaweed strips, diakon radish threads and a mound of grated wasabi horseradish. Sashimi is usually eaten at the beginning of a meal, as a light appetizer. Various dipping sauces and accompaniments are used to enhance the flavors of the fish.

There is a very old tradition in Japan of always serving sashimi with an odd number of slices, as on the facing page. We do not know how this tradition arose.

Garnishes for Sashimi

Decorate sashimi with leaves or leaf cutouts, cucumber decorations (page 14), wasabi and mounds of finely shredded daikon radish or carrot. Lemon also goes very well with most fish. Simply cut half slices or wedges of lemon and add them to the sashimi display.

Garnishes for sashimi: (Clockwise from top left) Shiso leaf, Cucumber decoration, Carrot decorations, Shredded seaweed, Shredded daikon on a shisho leaf, Shredded carrot

Tuna and Nori Sashimi Rolls

2 nori sheets, each 7 x 8 in (18 x 20 cm), quartered

8 oz (250 g) tuna fillet or other fish

Note: Rolls of this style can also be made by rolling tuna in flat sheets of diakon radish and then rolling avocado in tuna.

1 Cut the tuna fillet into 1 x 1 x 3-in (2.5 x 2.5 x 7.5-cm) logs. Lay a nori sheet, shiny-side down, on a bamboo rolling mat. Place 1 tuna log on the nori and roll up as per Sushi Roll method (page 47).

2 Place the tuna nori roll on a cutting board and slice into $1/2$-in (1-cm) thick slices.

Makes 8 rolls   Preparation time: 10 mins

Squid, Nori and Cucumber Rolls

8 oz (250 g) squid

2 nori sheets, each 7 x 8 in (18 x 20 cm)

1 Japanese cucumber

Makes 8 rolls
Preparation time: 20 mins

1 Cut the squid into a 2 x 4 x $1/4$-in (5 cm x 10 cm x 6 mm) sheet. Use a knife to score the squid at 1–2-in ($2^1/2$–5-cm) intervals along the length of the squid sheet. This will help you to roll it smoothly.

2 Cut the nori into 2–4-in (5–10-cm) sheets.

3 Cut the cucumber into $1/4$ x $1/4$ x 2-in (6-mm x 6-mm x 5-cm) sticks.

4 Lay the squid on a cutting board, scored-side down. Lay the nori on top, then place a cucumber slice on top. Roll up the squid into a roll, then slice it into $1/2$-in (12-mm) thick rounds.

How to Make a Decorative Fish Rose

You can make a rose out of sliced fish! Slice small, thin sheets of white fish, such as silvery skinned mackerel or sea bream (whiting) as shown in the photo. You can also use tuna or salmon for this. Roll one sheet into a tight roll to form the center. Roll another piece around it, and continue adding more sheets one at a time in this way until you have the size you require.

Nigiri Sushi

Nigiri Sushi is the type of sushi most often served in sushi bars. In Japanese, nigiri means "to squeeze." Nigiri Sushi are made by gently squeezing together bite-sized pieces of fish (or other foods) on top of small logs of sushi rice.

At sushi bars, you may notice that the sushi vary somewhat from chef to chef. The quantities of rice, wasabi and other ingredients differ a little, and the shapes of the rice and the toppings may also differ. The shapes are dictated by tradition, the chef's cooking style or the ingredients used. But the most important thing for the home cook is to make sushi that stick together well and stand up on the plate.

As your guide to size, remember that sushi is best eaten in a single mouthful, so for each piece of sushi use a ball of rice approximately the size of two fingers and enough topping to cover it. Use a moderate amount of wasabi for richer, more oily fish such as tuna and salmon, and less for mild-tasting seafood such as shrimp, squid and octopus. Wasabi is normally not added to egg or vegetable sushi.

There are three or four common methods for making Nigiri Sushi. You may find that your sushi chef uses a different method, but we recommend the simple style shown on the following pages, as it gives good results and, with a little practice, is easy to master.

When making sushi, always make sure that your hands are a little moist, so the rice does not stick to them. Keep a damp cloth handy for wiping knives, and a bowl of *tezu* (water mixed with a bit of rice vinegar) for keeping your hands moist. You may notice that your sushi chef has beautifully smooth hands. Both the oils from the fish and the acidity of the sushi vinegar in the *tezu* combine to moisturize and renew the skin.

Classic Nigiri Sushi

2 cups (240 g) Prepared Sushi Rice
($^1/_2$ of recipe on pages 22-23)
7 oz (200 g) raw fish (salmon or
tuna), sliced into 16 strips
measuring $2^1/_2$ x $1^1/_4$ x $^1/_4$-in
(6 x 3 x $^1/_2$-cm) or other toppings of your choice (such as
jumbo shrimp, page 34)
Wasabi paste, to taste
Pickled Ginger (page 25), to serve
Soy sauce, for dipping

Tezu Vinegar Water
1 cup (250 ml) water
2 tablespoons rice vinegar
1 teaspoon salt

Makes 16 sushi
Preparation time: 20 mins + time
for making Sushi Rice

1 Prepare the Sushi Rice by following the recipe on pages 22-23.
2 Combine the Tezu ingredients in a bowl and mix well.
3 To shape the rice, first moisten your hands in the bowl of Tezu to prevent the rice from sticking to your hands, then take 2 tablespoons of the Sushi Rice and shape it into an oval "finger", pressing it gently to form a small log. Pick up a slice of the topping using your left hand and dab a little wasabi (if using) on it with your right index finger.
4 Place the rice "finger" on top of the topping and press it onto the wasabi-dabbed topping with your index finger. Then turn the rice and topping over so that the topping is on top. Using your index finger and middle finger, mold the topping around the rice, press-ing it gently around the rice so that the rice does not show around the edges of the topping. Repeat with the remaining ingredients to make a total of 16 sushi.
5 Arrange the sushi on a serving platter and serve immediately with mounds of wasabi paste, Pickled Ginger and small dipping bowls of soy sauce.

Note: When purchasing fresh fish, make sure to check if the fish is good for eating raw. Buy only sushi-grade fish. Before using salmon, cover it with salt and marinate for 1 hour, then rinse off the salt and place it in the freezer. Once frozen, take it out from the freezer to defrost, then slice it for making sushi or sashimi.

Step-by step Nigiri Sushi

1 Wet your hands with Tezu and hold a slice of the topping with your left hand. Shape 2 tablespoons of the Sushi Rice into an oval "finger" with your right hand. Using the tip of your right index finger, dab a little wasabi, if using, on the topping.

2 Using your index finger, press the rice onto the wasabi-dabbed topping.

3 Turn the rice and topping over so that topping is on top. Using your index and middle fingers, mold the topping around the rice and gently press it down onto the rice, so that there is no rice showing around the edges.

4 Arrange the sushi on a serving platter and serve immediately.

Preparing Jumbo Shrimp for Nigiri Sushi

This is the method to use when preparing jumbo shrimp or king prawns for sushi. It will cook them just right and prevent them from curling.

1 Wash the shrimp under running water and discard the heads. Insert a bamboo skewer or a long toothpick into the shell of the underside of each shrimp, from its head to tail, running along the appendages without touching the flesh.

2 Bring a pot of salted water (use enough salt to make the water tastes like sea water) to a boil and add the shrimp. Do not cover the pot with a lid. After 3 to 5 minutes of boiling, the shrimp will turn pink and rise to the surface. To check if the shrimp are cooked, remove a shrimp from the pot and squeeze it gently. If the inside is firm, it means the shrimp is cooked, and you can remove all the shrimp from the pot. Immediately plunge the boiled shrimp into iced water. This will give them a good color and stop the flesh from shrinking and becoming hard. When the shrimp are cooled, remove them from the iced water and drain in a colander.

3 Gently remove the skewer or toothpick from each shrimp using a screwing motion to avoid breaking the flesh. Peel the shrimp but keep the tails intact.

4 Make a butterfly cut by laying each shrimp on a flat surface with its tail away from you and cutting along the belly, from the head to tail, with the knife only going halfway in. Then open out the shrimp using the knife or your fingers and flatten it gently without breaking the flesh. Remove the vein and rinse the shrimp with mildly salted water. Drain the shrimp on paper towels and use them to make Nigiri Sushi by following the recipe on page 32.

Note: For making Sushi Rolls (page 57) and Sushi in a Bowl (pages 70-75), remove and discard the tails, and cut the shrimp in half lengthwise, or leave them whole.

Omelette Nigiri Sushi

2 cups (240 g) Prepared Sushi Rice
  ($^1/_2$ of recipe on pages 22-23)
16 nori belts (optional)

Sushi Omelette
4 eggs
$^1/_3$ cup (85 ml) Dashi Soup Stock
  (page 90)
3 tablespoons sugar
1 teaspoon mirin
$^1/_2$ teaspoon salt
2 tablespoons soy sauce
Oil for greasing the pan

Makes 16 sushi
Preparation time: 10 mins + time
  for making Sushi Rice
Cooking time: 15 mins

1 Prepare the Sushi Rice by following the recipe on pages 22-23.

2 In a bowl, beat the eggs lightly. Add the Dashi Soup Stock, sugar, mirin, salt and soy sauce, and stir until the sugar is dissolved. Set aside.

3 Heat a square omelette pan over medium heat and grease it with a little oil. Pour in a thin layer of the omelette mixture, using chopsticks or a spatula to press out any air bubbles. When the omelette is firm, run the chopsticks around it to loosen, and fold $^1/_3$ of the omelette over the center $^1/_3$, then fold the other side to the middle to form a thick stack.

4 Pour in more omelette mixture, lifting the cooked omelette up to let the mixture flow underneath. When firm, fold the omelette over as before. Continue adding the omelette mixture, then cooking it and folding it until the omelette mixture is used up and a thick multi-layered rectangle is formed. Remove the omelette from the heat and use a wooden board that fits inside the pan or a spatula to press down and shape the omelette. Allow the omelette to cool before cutting or refrigerating.

5 To make the Nigiri Sushi slices as shown in the photo opposite, slice the omelette into sixteen $^1/_2$ x 1 x 3-in (1 x 3 x 7$^1/_2$-cm) pieces, then shape the sushi using the method described on pages 32 to 33. Dampen 1 end of each nori belt (if using) and use it to strap the omelette piece to the Sushi Rice log.

Note: Without the right equipment, it may be difficult to create an omelette of exactly the desired shape. Alternatively, cook the omelette, lay it on a bamboo rolling mat and use the mat to flatten and shape it. To make the thin, crepe-like omelette to be shredded and used for Chirashi Sushi (pages 70-75) or sliced for Sushi Rolls (page 57), heat and grease the pan, then pour in a thin layer of the omelette mixture and cook until firm. Remove from the heat and set aside to cool, then slice into fine shreds or thinly sliced.

Square Sushi with Seared Tuna

1 cups (120 g) Prepared Sushi Rice ($^1/_4$ of recipe on pages 22-23)

7 oz (200 g) fresh tuna, trimmed into a 2 x 2 x 4-in (5 x 5 x 10-cm) block

8 fresh chives (thin tips only)

$^3/_4$ x 2-in (2 x 5-cm) piece fresh ginger root, peeled and grated

Wasabi paste, to serve

Soy sauce, for dipping

1 Prepare the Sushi Rice by following the recipe on pages 22-23.

2 Fill a heatproof, nonmetallic bowl with boiling water. Immerse the tuna block in the boiling water to poach its surface for about 10 seconds. Transfer to a clean kitchen towel and pat dry. Alternatively, lightly pan-fry all 4 sides of the tuna block on a heated skillet with 1 teaspoon of olive oil in it. Set aside.

3 On a cutting board, use a sharp knife to slice the tuna block horizontally into 8 square pieces, each $^1/_2$ in (1 cm) thick.

4 Lay a piece of plastic wrap on a work surface. Wet a $2^1/_2$-in (6-cm) square mold and place it on the plastic wrap. Using a rice paddle, place 3 to 4 tablespoons of the Sushi Rice in the mold and press to conform. With wet hands, remove the square rice block from the mold. Continue with the remaining Sushi Rice to make 7 square rice blocks.

5 Place a blanched or seared tuna square on each rice block and tie a chive around it. Serve immediately with grated ginger, wasabi and soy sauce.

Makes 8 sushi
Preparation time: 30 mins + time for making Sushi Rice
Cooking time: 10 mins

Battleship Sushi (Gunkan Sushi)

Some ingredients will not stay on top of the sushi rice log by themselves, so with very soft ingredients such as sea urchin and salmon roe, it is necessary to wrap the sushi rice within nori sheets to hold it together. This is called gunkan ("battleship") sushi because it resembles tiny ships. When making gunkan sushi, remember that moist hands are good for touching the sushi rice, but it is best to have dry hands when handling the nori sheets as otherwise they absorb moisture and lose their stiffness. So, if you are making various kinds of sushi, leave the gunkan sushi for last.

2 cups (240 g) Prepared Sushi Rice ($^1/_2$ of recipe on pages 22-23)
1 portion Tezu Vinegar Water (page 32)
1 sheet nori, 7 x 8 in (18 x 20 cm)
Wasabi paste, to taste
4 oz (120 g) sea urchin, salmon roe, ocean trout roe or flying fish roe
Soy sauce, for dipping

1 Prepare the Sushi Rice by following the recipe on pages 22-23. Prepare the Tezu Vinegar Water as described on page 32.

2 Cut the nori sheet into 1 x 6-in ($2^1/_2$ x 15-cm) strips. Set aside.

3 To shape the rice, wet your hands in the bowl of Tezu, then take 2 tablespoons of the Sushi Rice and gently shape it into a log with rounded edges. Place it on a clean board. Repeat with the remaining rice to make a total of 16 rice logs.

4 With one moist hand holding a rice log, use your other dry hand to pick up a nori strip. Press one end of the nori strip to the rice and wrap the strip, rough side facing the rice, all around the rice log. Gently press the overlapping edge of the strip to seal, or use a crushed grain of sticky rice to hold the ends together. Continue to wrap the remaining rice logs with the nori strips in the same manner.

5 Dab each wrapped rice log with a little wasabi (if using), and cover the top with sea urchin or fish roe. Serve immediately with soy sauce and wasabi paste.

Makes 16 sushi
Preparation time: 20 mins + time for making Sushi Rice

Marinated Mackerel Sushi

This is a very traditional style of sushi and is wonderful to people who enjoy pickled herring, as the taste is quite similar. The fish is first marinated in a vinegar mixture and then used to make Nigiri Sushi. Because it is already seasoned, you may not need as much soy sauce for dipping. Marinating fish gives a different taste and color, and adds to the variety in a mixed sushi plate.

2 cups (240 g) Prepared Sushi Rice
  ($^{1}/_{2}$ of recipe on pages 22-23)
1 portion Tezu Vinegar Water
  (page 32)
16 mackerel strips, for topping
Salt as needed
Rice vinegar as needed
Wasabi paste, to taste
Pickled Ginger (page 25), to serve
Soy sauce, for dipping

1 Prepare the Sushi Rice by following the recipe on pages 22-23. Prepare the Tezu Vinegar Water as described on page 32.

2 Using the three-part filleting method (page 19), fillet the mackerel to obtain 16 mackerel sushi strips.

3 Wet some paper towels and squeeze out the water. Line the base of a flat-bottomed container with these towels and sprinkled with some salt. Lay the mackerel strips, skin-side down, on top of the salted paper and rub some salt into each. Marinate the strips for 2 hours if using small fish or 3 hours if using large fish.

4 Gently rinse salt off the mackerel strips, then drain them on clean, dry paper towels. Transfer to a bowl and pour in enough rice vinegar to cover. Set aside for 30 minutes if using small strips, or 1 hour if using large strips, then drain. If more fish flavor is preferred, reduce the soaking time. Wrap the marinated mackerel strips in plastic wrap and chill in the refrigerator overnight.

5 On the following day, use the fish to make Nigiri Sushi by following the steps described on pages 32-33. Make sure you have removed all the bones from the fish before using. Serve with wasabi paste, Pickled Ginger and soy sauce.

Makes 16 sushi
Preparation time: 30 mins + 3 hours to marinate + overnight chilling + time for making Sushi Rice

Sushi Rolls

Sushi rolls are a simple, easy-to-eat style of food—the Japanese equivalent of a sandwich. They are made by wrapping sushi rice and all sorts of other available ingredients in nori seaweed and shaping the rolls with a bamboo rolling mat. With a little practice, sushi rolls are quite easy to make.

Small sushi rolls (Maki Sushi) usually have only one type of filling plus the rice, as the roll is quite slender. Thick sushi rolls (Futomaki Sushi) have several ingredients in addition to the rice, and can even be rolled in a variety of ways to make decorative patterns in the rice. Experiment by laying the ingredients in differing patterns on the nori. For making sushi rolls, a bamboo rolling mat is essential. If you try using a length of cloth or plastic wrap instead, the results are likely to be disappointing.

The best-made sushi rolls have the filling exactly in the center, with the rice and nori in concentric circles around the filling. While preparing sushi rolls, keep the other ingredients, such as wasabi and sesame seeds, in a small dish near you so you can easily reach them when needed.

Judge carefully the amount of filling needed to place inside the rolls. If the rolls are over-filled, the sheets of nori are likely to break. If you want to add more ingredients to make a thicker roll, you will need to lay the nori sheet vertically on the rolling mat, giving you a larger area of nori to wrap around the ingredients.

Sushi rolls are always served with Pickled Ginger slices (*gari,* page 25) and individual bowls of soy sauce for dipping. The type of garnish used will depend on the fillings that have been used and on personal taste. For example, white sesame seeds and shiso leaves go particularly well with cucumber rolls.

Sushi rolls should be eaten as soon as possible after they have been made. Nori soon absorbs moisture and becomes soggy, rather like paper, and the rice inside also expands and may cause the nori to split. Sushi rolls will keep for up to 30 minutes if they are rolled in a paper towel and then in plastic wrap.

Classic Thin Tuna Rolls (Tekkamaki)

2 cups (240 g) Prepared Sushi Rice
($^1/_2$ of recipe on pages 22-23)
1 portion Tezu Vinegar Water
(page 32)
2 sheets nori, each 7 x 8 in (18 x
20 cm)
Wasabi paste, to taste
4 oz (120 g) fresh tuna, cut into 4
long thin strips, each $^1/_2$ x $^1/_2$ x 6
in (12 mm x 12 mm x 15 cm)

Makes 4 rolls (24 pieces)
Preparation time: 30 mins + time
for making Sushi Rice

1 Prepare the Sushi Rice by following the recipe on
pages 22-23. Prepare the Tezu as described on page 32.
2 Cut each nori sheet in half lengthwise, then trim 1 in
($2^1/_2$ cm) from both ends of each half sheet. You should
have 4 sheets, each measuring $3^1/_2$ x 6 in (9 x 15 cm).
3 To make the sushi rolls, place a nori sheet on a
bamboo rolling mat, shiny side down, about 1 in ($2^1/_2$
cm) from the edge of the mat closest to you and with
equal space on each end. Wet your hands in the bowl
of Tezu to avoid the rice from sticking, take a handful
of the Sushi Rice (about $^1/_2$ cup/60 g) and gently press
it into a flat rectangle. Place the rice in the center of
the nori sheet and gently press it down.

4 Spread the rice evenly over the nori, leaving a $^3/_4$-in (2-cm) strip along the top edge uncovered. Build a low ridge of rice in front of this uncovered strip.

5 Take a dab of wasabi on your finger and wipe it across the center of the rice. Place a tuna strip along the center of the rice, over the wasabi.

6 Place your fingers over the tuna strip to hold it in place, then use your thumbs to lift the edge of the rolling mat closest to you over the filling, forming it into a roll.

7 Roll the mat up, pressing all around to keep the roll firm.

8 Lift up the top of the rolling mat and turn the roll a little to overlap the edges of the nori and seal the roll. When the edges come in contact, they seal themselves.

9 Roll the entire roll once more, exerting gentle pressure to ensure it will keep its shape and remain sealed.

10 Slice the roll in half, then using a moist, very sharp knife, cut both halves to make 6 equal segments. Repeat with the remaining nori and rice.

Cucumber and Sesame Rolls

2 cups (240 g) Prepared Sushi Rice
($^1/_2$ of recipe on pages 22-23)
1 portion Tezu Vinegar Water
(page 32)
2 sheets nori, each 7 x 8 in (18 x
20 cm)
Wasabi paste, to taste
1 Japanese cucumber, cut into 4
long thin strips, each $^1/_4$ x $^1/_2$ x 6
in (6 mm x 12 mm x 15 cm)
2 teaspoons white sesame seeds

1 Prepare the Sushi Rice by following the recipe on pages 22-23. Prepare the Tezu as described on page 32.
2 Cut each nori sheet in half lengthwise, then trim 1 in ($2^1/_2$ cm) from both ends of each half sheet. You should have 4 sheets, each measuring $3^1/_2$ x 6 in (9 x 15 cm).
3 Make the sushi rolls by following the recipe on pages 46 to 47 (Step 3-10), using 1 cucumber strip with some sesame seeds added as the filling for each roll. Sprinkle the sesame seeds along the center of the rice before placing the cucumber strip in place.

Makes 4 rolls (24 pieces)
Preparation time: 30 mins + time for making Sushi Rice

Tuna and Cucumber Rolls

2 cups (240 g) Prepared Sushi Rice
($^1/_2$ of recipe on pages 22-23)
1 portion Tezu Vinegar Water
(page 32)
2 sheets nori, each 7 x 8 in (18 x
20 cm)
Wasabi paste, to taste
4 oz (120 g) fresh tuna, cut into 4
long thin strips, each $^1/_4$ x $^1/_2$ x 6
in (6 mm x 12 mm x 15 cm)
1 Japanese cucumber, cut into 4
long thin strips, each $^1/_4$ x $^1/_2$ x 6
in (6 mm x 12 mm x 15 cm)

1 Prepare the Sushi Rice by following the recipes on pages 22-23. Prepare the Tezu as described on page 32.
2 Cut each nori sheet in half lengthwise, then trim 1 in ($2^1/_2$ cm) from both ends of each half sheet. You should have 4 sheets, each measuring $3^1/_2$ x 6 in (9 x 15 cm).
3 Make the sushi rolls by following the recipe on pages 46 to 47 (Step 3-10), using 1 tuna strip and 1 cucumber strip as the filling for each roll.

Makes 4 rolls (24 pieces)
Preparation time: 30 mins + time for making Sushi Rice

California Rolls

California rolls, as their name suggests, were invented in California, although thick sushi rolls like these ones originated in the Osaka area of Japan.

4 cups (475 g) Prepared Sushi Rice (1 recipe on pages 22-23)
1 portion Tezu Vinegar Water
4 sheets nori
8 teaspoons flying fish roe
1 Japanese cucumber, cut into thin, lengthwise strips
4 jumbo shrimp or king prawns, cooked and peeled, deveined and halved lengthwise
1 ripe avocado, peeled, pitted and sliced lengthwise into thin strips

1 Prepare the Sushi Rice by following the recipe on pages 22-23. Prepare the Tezu as described on page 32.
2 Lay 1 nori sheet lengthwise on a bamboo rolling mat, shiny side down. Wet your hands in the bowl of Tezu to avoid the rice from sticking, take 1 cup (120 g) of the Sushi Rice and place it on the nori sheet.

Makes 4 rolls (32 pieces)
Preparation time: 30 mins + time for making Sushi Rice

3 Spread the rice evenly over the nori, leaving a $^3/_4$-in (2-cm) strip along the top edge uncovered. Build a low ridge of rice in front of this uncovered strip. This will keep the filling in place.

4 Spoon 2 teaspoons of the fish roe and spread it along the center of the rice.

5 Lay 2 shrimp pieces along the center end-to-end, along with several thin cucumber strips.

6 Lay strips of avocado along the center.

7 Roll the mat over once, pressing the ingredients in to keep the roll firm and leaving the strip of nori at the top edge free.

8 While covering the roll (but not the open strip of nori), hold the rolling mat in position and press all around to make the roll firm.

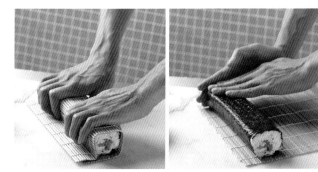

9 Lift up the top of the rolling mat and turn the roll over to overlaps the other edge of nori to seal the roll.
10 Roll the entire roll once more, and press to shape it. Using a sharp knife, cut each roll in half, then cut each half in half again. Then cut each quarter in half crosswise to make a total of 8 equal segments as shown at left.

Inside-out California Rolls

3 cups (360 g) Prepared Sushi Rice
($^3/_4$ of recipe on pages 22-23)
1 portion Tezu Vinegar Water
(page 32)
2 sheets nori, each 7 x 8 in (18 x
20 cm)
8 teaspoons flying fish roe
1 Japanese cucumber, cut into
thin, lengthwise strips
1 ripe avocado, peeled, pitted and
sliced lengthwise into thin strips
4 jumbo shrimp or king prawns,
cooked and peeled, deveined
and halved lengthwise

1 Prepare the Sushi Rice by following the recipe on pages 22-23, and the Tezu as described on page 32.
2 Cut each nori sheet in half lengthwise, then trim 1 in ($2^1/_2$ cm) from both ends of each half sheet. You should have 4 sheets, each measuring $3^1/_2$ x 6 in (9 x 15 cm).
3 Cover a rolling mat with a sheet of plastic wrap, folding it under the edges and attaching it to the back of the mat. Turn the mat over so the covered side is facing up. Place a nori sheet lengthwise on the mat.
4 Wet your hands in the bowl of Tezu and take a handful of the sushi rice (about $^3/_4$ cup/90 g) and gently press it into a flat rectangle. Place the rice on the nori sheet and gently press it down to flatten.

Makes 4 rolls (24 pieces)
Preparation time: 30 mins + time for making Sushi Rice

5 Spread the rice evenly over the nori right up to the edges. Using the back of a spoon, spread 2 teaspoons of the fish roe evenly over the rice.

6 Pick up the rice-covered nori by the corners, and quickly turn it over and place it upside down on the bamboo rolling mat.

7 Lay the sliced cucumber along the center of the nori sheet.

8 Add the avocado slices, followed by the shrimp pieces.

9 With your hands holding the base of the mat and pressing in on the ingredients with your fingers, roll the mat over the ingredients, leaving $^3/_4$ in (2 cm) of the nori at the far end.

10 Press gently to mold the roll together, then lift up the mat and roll back a little. Finally roll forward to seal the nori edges, applying gentle pressure to mold the completed roll into shape, either round, oval or square.

11 Using a moist sharp knife, slice the roll in half, then cut both halves to make 6 equal segments. Repeat with the remaining nori and rice.

Omelette Sushi Rolls

2 cups (240 g) Prepared Sushi Rice ($1/_2$ of recipe on pages 22-23)

1 portion Tezu Vinegar Water (page 32)

1 portion Seasoned Shiitake Mushrooms (page 73), finely minced

1 piece deep-fried tofu, seasoned (page 66-67) and thinly sliced

2 sheets nori, each 7 x 8 in (18 x 20 cm)

1 Japanese cucumber, thinly sliced lengthwise

Wasabi paste, to taste

Pickled Ginger (page 25), to serve

Soy sauce, for dipping

Seasoned Carrot

1 carrot, peeled and cut into long thin strips

$1/_3$ cup (85 ml) Dashi Soup Stock (page 90)

2 teaspoons sugar

1 teaspoon soy sauce

$1/_3$ teaspoon salt

Thin Seasoned Omelette

3 eggs

$1/_2$ teaspoon mirin

$1/_2$ teaspoon sugar

$/_4$ teaspoon salt

1 teaspoon oil

Makes 2 rolls (16 pieces)

Preparation time: 1 hour + time for making fillings and Sushi Rice

1 Prepare the Sushi Rice by following the recipe on pages 22-23, and the Tezu as described on page 32. Make the Seasoned Shiitake by following the recipe on page 73.

2 To make the Seasoned Carrot, combine all the ingredients in a small saucepan and bring to a boil. Reduce the heat to low and simmer uncovered until most of the sauce is absorbed and the carrot is tender, about 10 minutes. Remove the carrot and slice thinly.

3 To make the Thin Seasoned Omelette, combine the eggs, mirin, sugar and salt in a bowl and beat gently. Lightly grease an 8-in (20-cm) square or 9-in (23-cm) round skillet and heat over low heat until hot. Pour $1/_2$ of the egg mixture into the skillet to form a flat thin layer, tilting the pan to spread the mixture evenly. Break any air bubbles with chopsticks so the omelette lies flat. When the mixture is almost set, run chopsticks around the edges to loosen the omelette from the pan. Flip the omelette over and cook the other side for a few seconds. Remove the omelette from the pan. Continue to cook the remaining egg mixture to make another omelette. Set aside to cool.

4 In a large bowl, combine the Seasoned Shiitake Mushrooms, Seasoned Carrot, seasoned deep-fried tofu and Sushi Rice, and mix well.

5 Cover a bamboo mat with plastic wrap (page 52). Lay 1 Thin Seasoned Omelette on the mat and cover it with a sheet of nori. Wet your hands in the bowl of Tezu and spread 1 cup (120 g) of the Sushi Rice mixture evenly over the nori, leaving a 1-in ($2^1/_2$-cm) strip along the top edge uncovered. Lay $1/_2$ of the cucumber strips across the rice, making sure they extend to each end.

6 Pick up the mat and plastic wrap with your thumbs while holding the cucumber in place with the fingers, roll the omelette around the filling and seal the uncovered strip of nori along the top edge. Unroll the mat and plastic. Transfer the roll to a cutting board and place it seam side down. Repeat with the remaining ingredients to make another roll.

7 Using a sharp moist knife, cut each roll into 8 pieces, then serve with wasabi, Pickled Ginger and soy sauce.

Smoked Salmon and Cream Cheese Rolls

2 cups (240 g) Prepared Sushi Rice
  ($1/_2$ of recipe on pages 22-23)
1 portion Tezu Vinegar Water
  (page 32)
4 smoked salmon slices, each 4 x
  6 in (10 x 15 cm)
1 tablespoon cream cheese
$1/_4$ teaspoon Japanese chili powder
  (page 10)
12 green beans, blanched

Makes 4 rolls (24 pieces)
Preparation time: 20 mins + time
  for making Sushi Rice

1 Prepare the Sushi Rice by following the recipe on pages 22-23 and the Tezu as described on page 32.
2 To make the sushi, cover a rolling mat with plastic wrap (page 52). Lay a salmon slice lengthwise on the mat, from the edge closes to you, then spread the cream cheese along the center and sprinkle with Japanese chili powder.
3 Wet your hands with Tezu, take a handful of the Sushi Rice (about $1/_2$ cup/60 g) and spread it evenly over the salmon, leaving about $3/_4$-in (2-m) strip along the top edge uncovered. Place 3 green beans along the center of the rice, then roll up and cut into 6 equal pieces in the same way as instructed on page 47. Repeat with the remaining salmon and rice.

Futomaki with Egg

2 cups (240 g) Prepared Sushi Rice ($^1/_2$ of recipe on pages 22-23)
1 portion Tezu Vinegar Water (page 32)
1 portion Seasoned Shiitake Mushrooms (page 73)
2 sheets nori, each 7 x 8 in (18 x 20 cm)
Sushi Omelette (page 37), cut into four $^1/_2$ x 1 x 8-in (1 x 2 x 20-cm) strips
1 Japanese cucumber, cut into thin strips lengthwise
Wasabi paste, to serve
Soy sauce, for dipping

1 Prepare the Sushi Rice by following the recipe on pages 22-23. Prepare the Tezu as described on page 32. Make the Seasoned Shiitake by following the recipe on page 73.
2 Make the sushi by following the California Roll method on pages 50-51, using 1 omelette piece, several thin cucumber slices and half of the Seasoned Mushrooms for the filling of each roll. Serve the sushi with wasabi and soy sauce.

Makes 2 rolls (16 pieces)
Preparation time: 10 mins + time for making fillings and Sushi Rice

Cone Sushi Rolls (Temaki Sushi)

Temaki Sushi are the easiest type of sushi to make at home. They are do-it-yourself hand-rolled cones of nori filled with sushi rice and a variety of other ingredients. They make excellent party food. Simply prepare the fillings ahead of time and lay them out attractively in separate bowls or on one large platter on the table. Give your guests a little guidance on how to make the rolls and then let them make their own, encouraging them to experiment with different combinations of fillings. You may also wish to provide each of your guests with a moist hand towel. Japanese restaurants provide clean, damp hand towels for diners to wipe their hands on. (You can heat them in the microwave and roll them up like cigars for a truly authentic experience.)

See the following pages for ingredient combinations and suggestions, and step-by-step instructions on how to assemble the Cone Sushi Rolls.

Photo shows Temaki Sushi with salmon and shiso (right), and Temaki Sushi with tempura and lettuce leaf (left)

Classic Temaki Cone Sushi

2 cups (240 g) Prepared Sushi Rice ($^1/_2$ of recipe on pages 22-23)
1 portion Tezu Vinegar Water (page 32)
4 sheets nori, each 7 x 8 in (18 x 20 cm), halved lengthwise
Wasabi paste, to taste
Japanese mayonnaise

Choice of Fillings
• Sea urchin or salmon roe
• Salmon or tuna fillets (about 5 oz/150 g), cut into $^3/_8$ x $^3/_8$ x 3-in (1 x 1 x 7$^1/_2$-cm) sticks
• Jumbo shrimp or king prawns, cooked and peeled, deveined and halved lengthwise
• Cooked or smoked fish, cut into $^3/_8$ x $^3/_8$ x 3-in (1 x 1 x 7$^1/_2$-cm) sticks
• Sushi Omelette (page 37), cut into 3-in (7$^1/_2$-cm) strips
• Japanese cucumbers, cut into 3-in (7$^1/_2$-cm) lengths, then finely sliced lengthwise

• Unagi eel fillets, cut into $^3/_8$ x $^3/_8$ x 3-in (1 x 1 x 7$^1/_2$-cm) sticks
• Crabmeat sticks, cut diagonally into halves
• Blanched vegetables such as asparagus, snow peas, sliced onion and carrot
• Sliced or torn fresh leaves such as lettuce or shiso or mint and basil

1 Prepare the Sushi Rice by following the recipe on pages 22-23 and the Tezu as described on page 32.
2 To make the sushi, pick up a sheet of nori and hold it flat in your left hand, rough side up. Wet your right hand in the bowl of Tezu, take about 2 tablespoons of the Sushi Rice and spread it evenly on the left side of the nori. Make a groove along the middle of the rice for the fillings.

Makes 16 sushi
Preparation time: 30 mins + time for making fillings and Sushi Rice

3 Using a small spoon, spread a small amount of the wasabi paste and Japanese mayonnaise on the rice. Place the fish roe on top.

4 Arrange the other fillings in the center of the rice. Here, the filling is made up of 1 Japanese cucumber stick, 1 avocado slice and 1 crabmeat stick cut in half.

5 Wipe the hand that was used to place the rice and fillings on the nori to dry it. Fold the bottom left-hand corner of the nori over the fillings and tuck it under the other side, allowing the top to open out into a cone. Roll the remainder of the nori sheet into a cone-shaped sushi roll.

6 To seal the nori, wet the edge with a little water. When the edges come in contact, they will seal themselves.

California Cone Rolls

2 cups (240 g) Prepared Sushi Rice
($^1/_2$ of recipe on pages 22-23)
1 portion Tezu Vinegar Water
(page 32)
8 sheets nori, each 7 x 8 in (18 x
20 cm), halved lengthwise
Wasabi paste, to taste
Japanese mayonnaise
8 teaspoons flying fish roe
16 jumbo shrimp or king prawns,
cooked and peeled, deveined
2 ripe avocados, peeled, pitted and
sliced lengthwise into 16 strips
1 Japanese cucumber, cut into 3-in
($7^1/_2$-cm) lengths, then finely
sliced lengthwise
Pickled Ginger (page 25), to serve
Soy sauce, for dipping

1 Prepare the Sushi Rice by following the recipe on pages 22-23 and the Tezu as described on page 32.
2 Make the sushi by following the Temaki Cone Sushi method on pages 60-61, using 1 shrimp, 1 avocado strip and 1 cucumber slice as the filling for each cone sushi. Spread $^1/_2$ teaspoon of the fish roe over the rice before arranging the filling on top. Serve the sushi immediately with Pickled Ginger, wasabi and soy sauce.

Makes 16 sushi
Preparation time: 30 mins + time for making Sushi Rice

Unagi Cone Rolls

2 cups (240 g) Prepared Sushi Rice
($^1/_2$ of recipe on pages 22-23)
1 portion Tezu Vinegar Water
(page 32)
8 sheets nori, each 7 x 8 in (18 x
20 cm), halved lengthwise
Wasabi paste, to taste
Japanese mayonnaise
1 large piece unagi eel fillet, cut
into 32 strips measuring $^3/_8$ x
$^3/_8$ x 3-in (1 x 1 x $7^1/_2$-cm) each
1 Japanese cucumber, cut into 3-
in ($7^1/_2$-cm) lengths, then finely
sliced lengthwise
Pickled Ginger (page 25), to serve
Soy sauce, for dipping

1 Prepare the Sushi Rice by following the recipe on pages 22-23 and the Tezu as described on page 32.
2 Make the sushi by following the Temaki Cone Sushi method on pages 60-61, using 2 unagi strips and 3 cucumber slices as the filling for each cone sushi. Serve the sushi immediately with Pickled Ginger, wasabi and soy sauce.

Makes 16 sushi
Preparation time: 20 mins + time for making Sushi Rice

Tofu Pouch Sushi (Inari Sushi)

Inari Sushi is named after the Japanese god of grains. According to myth, foxes are the messengers of Inari and guard the Inari shrines. Perhaps these sushi are so named because their pointed shape resembles the ears of a fox.

Inari Sushi are a popular form of take-out food in Japan, and are always popular with foreigners. They have a unique and intriguing flavor—the deep-fried tofu being both savory and sweet. The basic technique for making this sushi can be adapted to make many variations. Deep-fried slices of tofu are sliced open and used as pouches for the wads of sushi rice.

The deep-fried tofu slices are called *aburage*. Do not try to prepare them yourself; you can obtain readymade cooked *aburage* from an Asian supermarket. The type of tofu used to make *aburage* differs from other tofu in that more coagulants have been used. It is sliced thinly, pressed to release moisture, then deep-fried twice. Before you use it, rinse it briefly in boiling water to remove as much oil as possible. As well as being ideal for making pouches, deep-fried tofu can be cut up like ordinary tofu and used in miso soup, in simmered foods and in noodle dishes.

Deep-fried tofu slices are either square or oblong, and can be sliced in a number of ways to form pouches. Square slices can be sliced diagonally to make triangular Inari Sushi. Oblong slices can be opened out by being cut down the two shorter sides and one long side, then rolled around a filling and tied with strings of cooked kampyo (page 11). If you open out a rectangular pouch and then fold the mouth inwards to about half the depth of the pouch, you can make inari that resemble little boats.

If you find it difficult to open the tofu bags, try rolling the sheets of *aburage* with a rolling pin or slapping them between your hands.

As with most other types of sushi, the filling can be varied to suit your taste or to accommodate what is seasonally available. Some people add nothing to the sushi rice; others like to flavor it with toasted sesame seeds, vinegared lotus root, hemp seeds, Japanese chili powder or prickly ash pepper or lemon zest.

Whatever fillings you choose, they will need to be finely chopped or sliced if they are to fit comfortably within the tofu pouch once they have been mixed with the sushi rice.

Simple Inari Sushi

2 cups (240 g) Prepared Sushi Rice
  ($^1/_2$ of recipe on pages 22-23)
1 portion Tezu Vinegar Water
8 pieces 2 x 4-in (5 x 10-cm)
  deep-fried tofu
1 cup (250 ml) Dashi Soup Stock
  (page 90)
2 tablespoons sugar
2 teaspoons sake
2 tablespoons soy sauce

1 Prepare the Sushi Rice by following the recipe on pages 22-23 and the Tezu as described on page 32.

Makes 16 sushi
Preparation time: 15 mins + time for making Dashi Soup Stock and Sushi Rice

2 Bring a saucepan of water to a boil. Add the deep-fried tofu slices and boil for about 2 minutes to remove the oil. Remove from the heat and drain, then squeeze out the water.

3 Combine the boiled tofu slices, Dashi Soup Stock, sugar, sake and soy sauce in a saucepan and mix well.

4 Cover the mixture with an aluminum foil sheet. Using a small knife, poke a few holes on the foil sheet to allow the steam to escape and to keep the tofu submerged in the sauce during cooking. Bring the ingredients to a boil, then reduce the heat to low and simmer for about 10 minutes. Remove from the heat and set aside to cool.

5 Drain the deep-fried tofu slices and squeeze out the sauce. Place each piece of tofu on a flat surface and gently roll with a rolling pin to loosen the center.

6 Cut each piece of the tofu into half. If using square tofu slices, cut each piece diagonally into 2 triangles.

7 Open up each half of the tofu to form a pouch.

8 Wet one hand with the Tezu and fill each pouch with 2 tablespoons of the Sushi Rice.

9 Wrap the edges of the pouch around the rice to form a sushi, and serve on a platter with the open side down.

Seasoned Inari Rolls

2 cups (240 g) Prepared Sushi Rice
  ($^1/_2$ of recipe on pages 22-23)
8 pieces deep-fried tofu
1 portion Tezu Vinegar Water
  (page 32)
8 strips pickled radish, each $^1/_2$
  x $3^1/_4$ in (1 x 8 cm)
2 tablespoons toasted sesame
  seeds
24 green onion leaves, blanched
  and drained, for tying

1 Prepare the Sushi Rice by following the recipe on pages 22-23. Prepare the Tezu as described on page 32.
2 Season the deep-fried tofu by following the method described on pages 66-67. Cut open the 2 short sides and one of the larger sides of each tofu piece and open them out to a sheet with the shorter side towards you, rough side up.
3 Wet your hands in the bowl of Tezu, take a small handful (4 tablespoons) of the Sushi Rice and spread it evenly on each tofu sheet, leaving a $^1/_2$-in (1-cm) strip along the edge close to you and a $^3/_4$-in (2-cm) strip on the top edge uncovered. Lay 1 radish strip across the center of the rice and sprinkle with sesame seeds.
4 Roll each tofu sheet up tightly and secure by tying 3 green onion leaves around it, about $^3/_4$ in (2 cm) apart. Slice each roll, between the ties, into 3 pieces. Serve some pieces facing up and some on their sides for variation.

Makes 8 rolls (24 pieces)
Preparation time: 30 mins + time for making Sushi Rice

Pickled Ginger Inari Rolls

2 cups (240 g) Prepared Sushi Rice
  ($^1/_2$ of recipe on pages 22-23)
2 tablespoons finely chopped
  Pickled Ginger (page 25)
3 green onions, leaf part only,
  finely sliced
1 portion Tezu Vinegar Water
  (page 32)
8 pieces seasoned deep-fried tofu
  (pages 66-67)
24 green onion leaves, blanched
  and drained, for tying

1 Prepare the Sushi Rice by following the recipe on pages 22-23, then fold the chopped Pickled Ginger and green onion through the Sushi Rice, and set aside. Prepare the Tezu as described in page 32.
2 Cut open the tofu pieces and make them into rolls by following the method described in the above recipe, using the ginger sushi rice mixture for the filling. Slice each roll in thirds.

Makes 8 rolls (24 pieces)
Preparation time: 30 mins + time for making Sushi Rice

Sushi in a Bowl (Chirashi Sushi)

Chirashi Sushi is a great one-dish sushi meal that is easy to prepare at home. Chirashi means "scattered," and this is what you do: Fill a bowl with sushi rice and then scatter the other ingredients decoratively over the rice. Almost any fish or vegetable toppings can be used—it is up to the cook's imagination as to what it contains. Chirashi Sushi is usually served in beautiful individual lacquered serving bowls and makes a meal on its own.

The following recipe uses mostly cooked ingredients, but chirashi sushi is often made with sashimi on top. If sashimi is used, the dish is either accompanied with individual dishes of soy sauce, into which you dip the sashimi, or soy sauce is used to season the entire dish.

Chirashi Sushi often contains ingredients that are not used in other forms of sushi, such as *kamaboko* (fish cakes), baby corn, bamboo shoots and lotus root. Other ingredients that go well with Chirashi Sushi are crab, avocado, carrot, green beans, bell peppers, green onions, unagi eel, squid, thick omelette slices, tofu, sardines and sesame seeds.

If you wish, you can season the sushi rice used for Chirashi Sushi with chopped vegetables, green peas, chopped fresh ginger, *gari* (pickled ginger slices), *soboro*, crumbled nori, toasted sesame seeds, tofu or strips of deep-fried tofu, or various sauces. The dish is then known as Bara Sushi.

Classic Chirashi Bowl Sushi

4 cups (480 g) Prepared Sushi Rice
(1 recipe on pages 22-23)
2 tablespoons shredded fresh
ginger or Pickled Ginger (*gari*)
2 tablespoons shredded nori
$1/_2$ cup (60 g) shredded Sushi
Omelette (page 37)
1 Japanese cucumber, thinly sliced
4 jumbo shrimp or king prawns,
cooked, peeled, deveined and
butterfly cut (page 24)
8 snow peas, blanched
4 oz (120 g) grilled unagi eel, cut
into bite-sized pieces
Carrot petals (page 25)

Seasoned Shiitake Mushrooms

4 dried shiitake mushrooms,
soaked in warm water until soft,
stems discarded, caps sliced into
strips
1 cup (250 ml) Dashi Soup Stock
(page 90)
3 tablespoons Japanese soy sauce
1 tablespoon caster sugar
1 tablespoon mirin

1 Prepare the Sushi Rice by following the recipe on pages 22-23.
2 Prepare the Seasoned Shiitake Mushrooms by combining the Dashi Soup Stock, soy sauce, sugar and mirin in a saucepan and bring to a boil over medium heat. Add the soaked mushroom strips and simmer for 10 minutes. Remove the mushroom strips from the sauce, drain and set aside.
3 Divide the Sushi Rice into 4 individual serving bowls and spread out the rice to make a flat bed, keeping it loosely packed. Add the topping ingredients one by one, sprinkling them to cover the rice and then on top of each other in layers (page 75): shredded ginger, Seasoned Shiitake Mushrooms, shredded nori and shredded Sushi Omelette. Then make a decorative display on top with the cucumber, shrimp, snow peas, and unagi eel pieces.

Serves 4
Preparation time: 30 mins + time for making fillings
and Sushi Rice

Adding Ingredients to the Chirashi Sushi Rice Bowl

1 In a large bowl, spread Sushi Rice to make a flat bed, keeping the rice loosely packed. Add a layer of fresh ginger strips or Pickled Ginger, covering rice.

2 Add a layer of Seasoned Shiitake Mushrooms to cover ingredients already in the bowl. Grated dried fish (*soboro*) or bonito flakes may also be added.

3 Add a layer of shredded nori seaweed and shredded Sushi Omelette to cover the ingredients already in the bowl.

4 Make a decorative arrangement on top with the jumbo shrimp and snow peas. Finish off by adding carrot and cucumber slices for decoration.

Suggested Chirashi Sushi Ingredients

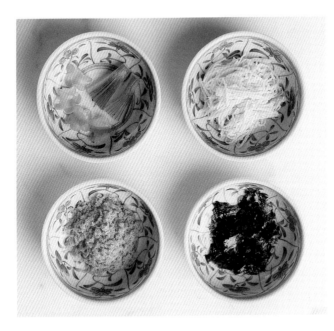

(Clockwise from back left)
carrot and cucumber slices,
shredded thin omelette,
shredded nori seaweed,
soboro (dried ground fish)

(Clockwise from back left)
Seasoned Kampyo (bottle
gourd), jumbo shrimp and
snow peas, Pickled Ginger,
Seasoned Shiitake
Mushrooms

Vegetable Sushi

Japanese people always favor using foods that are in season for their cooking, and the variety of vegetables available through the year provides great scope for the imaginative sushi maker. Vegetables combine well with the delicate flavor of sushi rice, as do various other foods, such as omelettes, tofu and cream cheese.

If you are making a mixed platter of sushi, it is a good idea to make a few vegetable sushi to add color and nutritional value. You can experiment with grilled, blanched and raw vegetables and various garnishes.

Vegetables also offer an economical alternative to expensive fish and seafood, which may sometimes be beyond the average household budget.

Experiment with garnishes such as fresh ginger, finely chopped shallots, miso paste and chili seasonings. You can also "Westernize" your sushi with your own variations, using all sorts of ingredients you already have in your kitchen.

Vegetable sushi often need to be wrapped with a nori belt to prevent the vegetables from falling off the sushi rice. You can use the scraps of nori from making sushi rolls or cut nori sheets into the appropriate lengths.

Tofu Sushi

2 cups (240 g) Prepared Sushi Rice
($1/_2$ of recipe on pages 22-23)
1 portion Tezu Vinegar Water
(page 32)
1 large cake firm tofu, drained
16 nori belts
Wasabi paste, to serve
Soy sauce, for dipping
Grated fresh ginger and minced
green onion, to garnish

1 Prepare the Sushi Rice by following the recipe on pages 22-23. Prepare the Tezu as described on page 32.
2 Cut the tofu into 16 pieces measuring $1/_4$ x $1 1/_2$ x 2 $1/_2$-in (6-mm x 4-cm x 6-cm) each.
3 Make the sushi by following the Nigiri Sushi method on pages 32-33, using 1 piece of tofu for the topping of each sushi.
4 Dampen 1 end of each nori belt and wrap it around the sushi to strap the topping to the Sushi Rice log. Serve the sushi with wasabi and soy sauce, garnished with grated fresh ginger and minced green onion.

Makes 16 sushi
Preparation time: 20 mins + time for making Sushi Rice

Avocado Sushi

2 cups (240 g) Prepared Sushi Rice
($1/_2$ of recipe on pages 22-23)
1 portion Tezu Vinegar Water
(page 32)
1 ripe avocado, peeled, pitted and
thinly sliced
16 nori belts
Wasabi paste, to serve
Soy sauce, for dipping
White or red miso paste, to garnish

1 Prepare the Sushi Rice by following the recipe on pages 22-23. Prepare the Tezu as described on page 32.
2 Make the sushi by following the Nigiri Sushi method on pages 32-33, using 2 slices of avocado for the topping of each sushi.
3 Dampen 1 end of each nori belt and wrap it around the sushi to strap the topping to the Sushi Rice log. Top each sushi with a dab of miso paste and serve with wasabi and soy sauce.

Makes 16 sushi
Preparation time: 20 mins + time for making Sushi Rice

Asparagus Sushi

2 cups (240 g) Prepared Sushi Rice
($^1/_2$ of recipe on pages 22-23)
1 portion Tezu Vinegar Water
(page 32)
16 asparagus spears, trimmed and
cut into 3-in (7-cm) lengths,
blanched and dipped in iced
water
16 nori belts
Mayonnaise or red miso paste,
to garnish
Wasabi paste, to serve
Soy sauce, for dipping

1 Prepare the Sushi Rice by following the recipes on pages 22-23. Prepare the Tezu as described on page 32.
2 Make the sushi by following the Nigiri Sushi method on pages 32-33, using 2 or 3 lengths of asparagus for the topping of each sushi.
3 Dampen 1 end of each nori belt and wrap it around the sushi to strap the topping to the Sushi Rice log. Top each sushi with a dab of mayonnaise or red miso paste. Serve the sushi with wasabi and soy sauce.

Makes 16 sushi
Preparation time: 20 mins + time for making Sushi Rice

Snow Pea Sushi

2 cups (240 g) Prepared Sushi Rice
($^1/_2$ of recipe on pages 22-23)
1 portion Tezu Vinegar Water
(page 32)
32 snow peas, ends trimmed,
then blanched and drained
16 nori belts
Mayonnaise or red miso paste, to
garnish
Wasabi paste, to serve
Soy sauce, for dipping

1 Prepare the Sushi Rice by following the recipe on pages 22-23. Prepare the Tezu as described on page 32.
2 Make the sushi by following the Nigiri Sushi method on pages 32-33, using 2 snow peas for the topping of each sushi.
3 Dampen 1 end of each nori belt and wrap it around the sushi to strap the topping to the Sushi Rice log. Top each sushi with a dab of mayonnaise or red miso paste. Serve the sushi with wasabi and soy sauce.

Makes 16 sushi
Preparation time: 20 mins + time for making Sushi Rice

Spinach and Brown Rice Sushi Rolls

1 portion Tezu Vinegar Water
(page 32)
5 oz (150 g) spinach leaves,
washed and then blanched and
drained well
$^1/_2$ teaspoon soy sauce
2 green onions, leaf part only,
finely chopped
1 tablespoon toasted white
sesame seeds
2 sheets nori, each 7 x 8 in (18 x
20 cm)

Brown Sushi Rice
1 cup (200 g) uncooked short-
grain brown rice
$^1/_2$ cup (125 ml) water

Sushi Rice Vinegar Sauce
3 tablespoons rice vinegar
$1^1/_2$ tablespoons sugar
$^1/_3$ teaspoon salt

Miso Sesame Sauce
4 tablespoons rice vinegar
2 tablespoons water or Dashi
Soup Stock (page 90)
1 tablespoon white miso paste
1 tablespoon sesame seed paste
or tahini
1 tablespoon sugar
1 teaspoon toasted white sesame
seeds
Thinly sliced green onion tops

1 Cook the Brown Sushi Rice by following the white rice method on page 22, using the brown rice and water mentioned here in place of the white Sushi Rice ingredients. If cooking without using the rice cooker, allow the cooked rice to steam in the covered pot for 10 to 15 minutes longer. Using the ingredients listed here, prepare the Sushi Rice Vinegar Sauce and add it to the cooked Brown Sushi Rice following the method described for white Rice on page 23.
2 Prepare the Tezu as described on page 32.
3 Make the Miso Sesame Sauce by combining the rice vinegar, water or Dashi Soup Stock, miso paste, sesame seed paste and sugar in a small bowl and stir until the sugar is dissolved. Cover and refrigerate until required. Sprinkle the top with white sesame seeds and green onion before serving.
4 Chop the blanched spinach leaves finely and sprinkle with the soy sauce, then divide into 4 equal portions and set aside.
5 Add the chopped green onion and sesame seeds to the sushi rice, and mix until evenly distributed.
6 Cut each nori sheet in half lengthwise, then trim 1 in ($2^1/_2$ cm) from both ends of each sheet. You should have 4 sheets, each measuring $3^1/_2$ x 6 in (9 x 15 cm).
7 Following the method on pages 46-47 (Step 3-10), use $^1/_2$ cup (60 g) of the Brown Sushi Rice and 1 portion of the seasoned spinach for the filling of each roll of sushi. Cut each roll into 6 pieces and serve with a bowl of Miso Sesame Sauce on the side.

Makes 4 rolls (24 pieces)
Preparation time: 30 mins + time for making Sushi Rice

Grilled Shiitake Sushi

2 cups (240 g) Prepared Sushi Rice
($1/2$ of recipe on pages 22-23)
1 portion Tezu Vinegar Water
(page 32)
1 tablespoon soy sauce
1 tablespoon mirin
16 fresh shiitake mushrooms,
stems discarded
16 nori belts
Wasabi paste, to serve
Soy sauce, for dipping

Makes 16 sushi
Preparation time: 25 mins + time
for making Sushi Rice

1 Prepare the Sushi Rice by following the recipe on pages 22-23. Prepare the Tezu as described on page 32.
2 Combine the soy sauce and mirin in a small bowl and mix well, then brush the mixture on the mushroom caps. Grill or broil the mushroom caps for 2 to 3 minutes, or until tender.
3 Make the sushi by following the Nigiri Sushi method on pages 32-33, using 1 mushroom cap for the topping of each sushi and placing it either upside-down or right-side up.
4 Dampen 1 end of each nori belt and wrap it around the sushi to strap the topping to the Sushi Rice log. Serve the sushi with wasabi and soy sauce.

Grilled Eggplant Sushi

2 cups (240 g) Prepared Sushi Rice
($1/2$ of recipe on pages 22-23)
1 portion Tezu Vinegar Water
(page 32)
2 Japanese eggplants
Oil, for basting
White sesame seeds, to garnish

Sweet Soy Sauce
$1/2$ cup (125 ml) soy sauce
2 tablespoons sugar
1 cup (250 ml) mirin

Makes 16 sushi
Preparation time: 30 mins + time
for making Sushi Rice
Cooking time: 20 mins

1 Prepare the Sushi Rice by following the recipe on pages 22-23. Prepare the Tezu as described on page 32.
2 To make the Sweet Soy Sauce, combine all the ingredients in a small saucepan, mix well and bring to a boil. Reduce the heat to low and simmer uncovered for 15 to 20 minutes until the sauce reduces to about 1 cup (250 ml) or $1/2$ cup (125 ml) if preferred. Set aside.
3 Slice the eggplant diagonally into sixteen $1/4$ x $1^1/_2$ x 2 $^1/_2$-in (6-mm x 4-cm x 6-cm) slices. Brush the eggplant slices with a little oil and grill on a grilling pan or under a broiler for about 2 minutes on both sides, or until tender and cooked. Allow to cool.
4 Make the sushi by following the Nigiri Sushi method on pages 32-33, using 1 eggplant slice for the topping of each sushi. Spread a little Sweet Soy Sauce on top of each sushi and sprinkled with a little sesame seeds. Serve immediately.

Vegetarian Cone Sushi

2 cups (240 g) Prepared Sushi Rice
($^1/_2$ of recipe on pages 22-23)
1 portion Tezu Vinegar Water
(page 32)
1 large carrot, peeled
1 piece daikon radish 6 in (15 cm)
long, peeled
$^1/_2$ teaspoon wasabi paste
(optional)
16 small beetroot or lettuce
leaves
8 sprigs radish sprouts (*kaiware*)
or alfalfa sprouts
8 sprigs enoki mushrooms with
stems
Balsamic vinegar, for dipping

Note: Radish sprouts are available
in Japanese markets.

1 Prepare the Sushi Rice by following the recipe on pages 22-23. Prepare the Tezu as described on page 32.
2 Using a vegetable shaver or mandolin, shave 16 very thin long wide strips from the thick top portion of the carrot and 8 very thin long wide strips from the daikon. These will be used as wrappers for the sushi so make them as wide and thin as possible. Alternatively, use 4 sheets of nori seaweed cut into half.
3 Place 1 strip of the carrot lengthwise on a flat surface and cover it with 1 strip of diakon on top. Place another strip of the carrot on top of the diakon strip so they overlap slightly, offsetting by about 1 in ($2^1/_2$ cm). Wet you hands in the bowl of Tezu and spread 2 table-spoons of the Sushi Rice evenly on the left side of the vegetable strips.
4 Spread the rice with a small amount of wasabi (if using) and place 2 beetroot or lettuce leaves, 1 sprig radish sprout and 1 sprig enoki mushrooms over the wasabi in the center of the rice. Using the method described on page 60, roll up the vegetable strips and its filling to form a cone. If preferred, wrap the cone in a 4 x 8-in (10 x 20-cm) rectangle of plastic wrap to hold it closed, but remember to remind your guests to remove it before eating. Continue to wrap the remaining ingredients into cones in the same manner.
5 Serve the cone sushi with balsamic vinegar in small dipping bowls, or black Chinese vinegar.

Makes 8 sushi
Preparation time: 20 mins + time for making Sushi Rice

Soups

There are two basic soups served with Japanese meals. One is the well-known miso, the other is a clear soup called *suimono*. To make both, begin with a stock called *dashi*. *Dashi* is also the basic ingredient in many other Japanese soups, sauces and traditional dishes and is used in the same way as Western-style stocks and consommés. It has a delicate, mildly fishy flavor. Traditional *dashi* is made with bonito fish that has been smoked, dried and fermented for several months so that it has the aroma and flavor of a fine air-dried ham. The hard bonito is shaved into flakes on a wooden block and steeped in water with a piece of *kombu*, or dried kelp. People generally use already prepared bonito flakes these days, which are sold in plastic packets and come in many different grades. Instant *dashi* stock powder or granules are also very popular in Japan now since they save a lot of time, although the flavor is not the same. But when making small quantities of *dashi* to be used in sauces, instant granules are perfectly acceptable.

We recommend making your own *dashi* using the traditional methods and ingredients because of the quality of the final stock, but as bonito flakes are not cheap and making *dashi* takes time, instant *dashi* (*hon dashi*) may be substituted.

The miso paste you use and other ingredients you add will determine the strength of the soup's flavor. Lighter-colored miso pastes generally have a subtle, slightly sweet flavor, whereas the darker brown, or "red" miso pastes have a saltier, stronger flavor. Experiment with different miso pastes in differing amounts until you find the style that suits you best.

Miso Soup with Tofu

Miso can be added to taste as some people like a saltier, heartier soup while others prefer this soup to be clear and delicate. Add almost any vegetable, meat or seafood to the soup, but be sparing with strongly flavored ingredients. Wakame seaweed, baby clams or cooked bamboo shoots make excellent additions. If the ingredients need cooking, cook them separately and then add to the finished soup.

4 cups (1 liter) Dashi Soup Stock
$1/_2$ cake soft tofu (5 oz/150 g)
2 tablespoons miso paste
1 green onion, leaf part only, very thinly sliced
$1/_2$ cup (5 g) dried wakame seaweed (optional)

Makes 4 cups (1 liter)
Preparation time: 10 mins
Cooking time: 5 mins

1 Bring the Dashi Soup Stock to a boil in a saucepan. Cube the soft tofu. Add the tofu cubes to the stock and simmer over low heat.
2 Scoop out a small amount of soup and dissolve the miso paste in it, then strain. Pour the clear stock to the simmering soup and stir to mix well, adjusting the taste with more miso if preferred. Do not boil the soup after adding the miso. Remove from the heat, add the green onion and wakame seaweed (if using) and serve hot.

Dashi Soup Stock

Dashi Soup Stock is best prepared on the day it is to be served, but it can be cooled, refrigerated and used the following day.

One 4-in (10-cm) square *kombu*
4 cups (1 liter) water
$1/_2$ cup (15 g) bonito flakes

Note: You can vary the amounts of *kombu* and bonito flakes to suit your taste. For vegetarian *dashi*, omit the bonito flakes and double the quantity of *kombu*.

Makes 4 cups (1 liter)
Preparation time: 5 mins
Cooking time: 10 mins

1 Wipe the *kombu* with a clean, damp cloth. Do not wash it as that will remove much of the flavor. In a saucepan, soak the *kombu* in the water for 1 to 2 hours.
2 Bring the mixture to a boil over low heat. Just before boiling, check the *kombu*. If it is soft, remove it from the stock and discard. If it is still hard, continue simmering for a few more minutes, then remove. Skim off any scum on the surface of the stock and remove from the heat.
3 Add some cold water to the stock to cool it, then add the bonito flakes. (Bonito flakes should never be cooked, only steeped in very hot water; they otherwise become "burnt".) Do not stir. Use chopsticks to press them down into the stock and allow them to steep for 3 minutes.
4 Strain the stock to remove the bonito flakes. Reserve the clear stock to be used as the base for Miso Soup (above) or Clear Soup (page 93).

Grilled Scallops and Salmon Roe in Miso Soup

1 tablespoon mirin
12 shucked fresh scallops
1 tablespoon oil
4 cups (1 liter) water
1$^1/_2$ tablespoons white miso paste
4 teaspoons salmon roe
1 green onion, leaf part halved
  lengthwise and tied into knots,
  to garnish

Serves 4
Preparation time: 20 mins

1 Drizzle the mirin over the scallops and set aside to marinate. Heat the oil in a grill pan or skillet over medium heat and grill or fry the scallops on each side until opaque. Do not overcook.
2 In a saucepan, bring the water to a boil, then simmer over low heat. In a small bowl, dissolve the miso paste in some boiling water, then pour the mixture into the saucepan. Add the cooked scallops and simmer for 1 to 2 minutes. Remove the soup from the heat.
3 Spoon 3 scallops into each serving bowl and ladle the soup over them. Top one of the scallops in each bowl with 1 teaspoon of the salmon roe. Serve the soup hot, garnished with green onion.

Carrot Tofu Clear Soup

1 piece carrot 4 in (10 cm) long,
  very thinly sliced
3 oz (100 g) green chives (about
  12), cut into 4-in (10-cm)
  lengths
$^1/_2$ cake firm tofu (5 oz/150 g),
  drained and diced
1 portion (4 cups/1 liter) Dashi
  Soup Stock (page 90)
1 teaspoon sake
1–2 teaspoons Japanese soy
  sauce, or to taste
$^1/_3$ teaspoon salt, or to taste
1 teaspoon finely chopped lemon
  peel or lemon curls, to garnish

Serves 4
Preparation time: 10 mins + time
  for making Dashi Soup Stock

1 Blanch the carrot slices in boiling water until cooked but still crisp, 1 to 2 minutes, then remove from the heat and drain. Alternatively, microwave the carrot slices in a covered container with 1 tablespoon of water on medium heat for about 2 minutes. Loosely knot the lengths of chives together in bunches of 4. Divide the carrot slices, chive knots and tofu equally in 4 serving bowls.
2 In a saucepan, bring the Dashi Soup Stock just to a boil over medium heat, then season with the sake, soy sauce and salt. Remove from the heat and carefully ladle the soup into the 4 serving bowls. Garnish with lemon peel and serve hot.

Easy Reference Table for Sushi Servings

Sushi type	Fillings	Nori	Sushi rice (cooked)
Nigiri Sushi (Topping on rice log)	1 slice or topping		2 tablespoons (8 per cup)
Battleship Sushi (Gunkan Maki Sushi)	1 topping	1 strip 1 x 5 in (2 x 3 cm)	2 tablespoons (2 teaspoons for mini size)
Thin Sushi Roll (Maki Sushi)	1–2 fillings	$^1/_2$ sheet	$^1/_2$ cup
California Roll (Futomaki Sushi)	5–6 fillings	1 sheet	1 cup
Inside-out Sushi Roll	3–4 fillings	$^1/_2$ sheet	$^3/_4$ cup
Cone Sushi (Temaki Sushi)	2–4 fillings	$^1/_4$ or $^1/_2$	2 tablespoons (8 per cup)
Seasoned Tofu Pouches (Inari Sushi)			4 tablespoons (4 per cup)

Suggested individual mixed sushi plates

4 Nigiri Sushi
1 Thin Sushi Roll (6 pieces)
2 Battleship Sushi (Gunkan Maki Sushi)
1 Seasoned Tofu Pouch (Inari Sushi)

OR

1 Thin Sushi Roll (6 pieces)
$^1/_2$ California Roll (4 pieces)
2 Seasoned Tofu Pouches (Inari Sushi)

Type of Sushi (1 cup Prepared Sushi Rice = 120 g)		Sushi for 2	Sushi for 4	Sushi for 6–8
To make Nigiri Sushi		20 pieces	40 pieces	60–80 pieces
(Topping on rice log)	Sushi rice needed	$2^1/_2$ cups	5 cups	$7^1/_2$–10 cups
	Toppings	20 slices	40 slices	60–80 slices
To make Battleship Sushi		12	24	36–48
(Gunkan Maki Sushi)	Sushi rice needed	$1^1/_2$ cups	3 cups	$4^1/_2$–6 cups
To make Thin Sushi Roll		4 rolls	8 rolls	12–16 rolls
(Maki Sushi)	(1 roll=6 pieces)	(24 pieces)	(48 pieces)	(72–96 pieces)
	Sushi rice needed	2 cups	4 cups	6–8 cups
		($1/_2$ portion)	(1 portion)	($1^1/_2$ portions)
	Nori sheets needed	2	4	6–8
	Fillings added	4 x 1-2 strips	8 x 1-2 strips	12–16 x 1-2 strips
To make California Roll		2 rolls	4 rolls	6–8 rolls
(Thick Sushi/Futomaki Sushi)	(1 roll=8 pieces)	(16 pieces)	(32 pieces)	(48–64 pieces)
	Sushi rice needed	2 cups	4 cups	6-8 cups
		($1/_2$ portion)	(1 portion)	($1^1/_2$ portions)
	Nori sheets needed	2	4	6–8
	Fillings added	2 x 5–6 strips	4 x 5–6 strips	6–8 x 5–6 strips
To make Inside-out Sushi Roll		4 rolls	8 rolls	12–16 rolls
	(1 roll=6 pieces)	(24 pieces)	(48 pieces)	(72-96 pieces)
	Sushi rice needed	3 cups	6 cups	9–12 cups
	Nori sheets needed	2	4	6–8
	Fillings added	4 x 3-4 strips	8 x 3-4 strips	12–16 x 3-4 strips
To make Cone Sushi		12	24	36–48
(Temaki Sushi)	Sushi rice needed	2 cups	4 cups	6–8 cups
	Fillings added	12 x 2–4	24 x 2–4	36–48 x 2–4
To make Seasoned	Number of pouches	6	12	18–24
Tofu Pouches	Sushi rice needed	$1^1/_2$ cups	3 cups	$4^1/_2$–6 cups
(Inari Sushi)	4 tablespoons per pouch (4 per cup)	(24 tablespoons)	(48 tablespoons)	(72–96 tablespoons)

Complete List of Recipes